STUDENT BODY
(College Edition)

Frank Winters

BROADWAY PLAY PUBLISHING INC
224 E 62nd St, NY, NY 10065
www.broadwayplaypub.com
info@broadwayplaypub.com

First printing: July 2016
I S B N: 978-0-88145-672-1

Book design: Marie Donovan
Typographic controls: Adobe InDesign
Typeface: Palatino
Printed and bound in the U S A

AUTHOR'S NOTE

When this play was first commissioned by The
Strasberg Institute, it was for a group of young
actors, and so was set it in a high school. When it
was subsequently produced at The Flea Theatre, we
decided to make the characters a few years older, as
their resident acting company, The Bats, were mostly
in their middle or late 20s. The shift of the setting
from high school to college required a reimagining
of a number of characters, relationships, and group
dynamics. Beyond that, each version of the play
reflects the work of the different actors, designers and
production teams this play enjoyed, particularly that
of directors Michelle Tattenbaum, Danny Sharron, and
associate director Alex Keegan. So, now we have these
two utterly similar, yet wildly different plays, existing
in alternate realities right next to each other within the
multiverse of the American Theater. Enjoy.

STUDENT BODY (College Edition) was originally commissioned, developed and performed at the Lee Strasberg Theatre and Film Institute in New York City as part of the Clifford Odets Ensemble Play Commission in December 2014 under the title THE SCHOOL PLAY.

STUDENT BODY (College Edition) was produced at
The Flea Theater as STUDENT BODY, running from
11 October–8 November 2015. The cast and creative
contributors were:

APRIL .... Comfort Katchy
DAISY .... Mariette Strauss
LUCY .... Daniela Rivera
MALCOLM.. Alex J Gould
NATALIE .... Audrey Wang
LIZ .... Alesandra Nahodil
PETE .... Adam Alexander Hamilton
ROB .... Tommy Bernardi
MAGGIE .... Sydney Blaxill
SARAH.. Alexandra Curran
Understudies .... Jessie Cannizzaro, Olivia Jampol
                                             Jack Horton Gilbert
Director .... Michelle Tattenbaum
Scenic designer............................... Jerad Schomer
Lighting designer .... Elizabeth M Stewart
Costume designer .... Stephanie Levin
Sound designer................................. Lee Kinney
Fight choreographer .... John L Puma
Props master .... Hye Young Chyun
Production technical director.............. Conor Moore
Production stage manager .... Kaila Hill
Rehearsal stage manager..................... Eh-Den Perlove

CHARACTERS & SETTING

APRIL
DAISY
LUCY
MALCOLM
NATALIE
LIZ
PETE
ROB
MAGGIE
SARAH

A black box theater at Craigstown University

AUTHOR'S OTHER NOTE

Use of the "/" means this is where the next line begins, overlapping with the preceding line's dialogue.

(The lights come up on a little black box theater tucked away in a corner of Craigstown University, behind the art building and letting out into the parking lot commonly known as "D2". At rise, the theater is littered with the detritus of tech week. There's paint cans and lights and gobos and a ladder—lumber sticking out of a re-purposed garbage can. After Christmas break, they'll be doing something like Brecht's The Good Person of Szechwan. APRIL, *a stage manager, enters, sees the mess, and sighs:)*

APRIL: Oh, come on, guys.

*(*APRIL *starts cleaning up. After a few moments, she gets a text that makes her smile, and then another. And then another.* DAISY *enters.)*

DAISY: Hello?

APRIL: Please don't touch anything please.

DAISY: Hi.

APRIL: Sorry—hi—just please don't touch anything made of sharp—look at this, would you look at this?

DAISY: What is it?

APRIL: It's a sharp—thing—that could stab you and give you tetanus. Which is bad. Do you know how you die from tetanus? You get Lockjaw. Do you want Lockjaw, Daisy?

DAISY: No.

APRIL: Yeah, well, me neither, which is exactly why—

DAISY: April, what is going on?

APRIL: I leave them alone for two seconds.

DAISY: I see.

APRIL: Two seconds so I could go back to my room and *not* find the scarf, / but apparently that's too much to ask, like, I walk out of here and it's recess. My God.

DAISY: Oh, I got your text before I left, was it this one? Hello? April? Was it this one?

APRIL: Yes! Thank you. Where was it?

DAISY: Under the couch. I tried to get the cat hair off, but.

APRIL: This is perfect. Thank you. And you're still coming tonight, right?

DAISY: Actually.

APRIL: Great. Glad to hear it.

DAISY: Seriously, though, I've actually, I've got these other plans.

APRIL: Like what?

DAISY: Doing literally anything else.

APRIL: Daisy, come on. It's freezing outside, and besides, there's somebody I really want you to meet. Come get drunk with me. Pleee/eeeeease? Please please.

LUCY: *(Off-stage)* Hello?

DAISY: Okay, fine.

APRIL: Thank you.

(DAISY *puts her bag down. Relents.* APRIL *smiles and takes off the sweatshirt she's been wearing.* LUCY *enters.*)

LUCY: April?

APRIL: Hey, Lucy.

(LUCY *takes in the weirdness of the half-finished set.*)

LUCY: Hi. What, um. The fuck is this place?

APRIL: Oh, do you like it? It's for the play we're doing after the break.

LUCY: It's nice.

APRIL: Thanks.

LUCY: Is Sarah here yet?

APRIL: You're the first. Lucy, do you know Daisy?

LUCY: Yeah, you were in Orgo with me, right? Last semester?

APRIL: No, Daisy doesn't know go to school here.

DAISY: You come into the Starbucks sometimes.

LUCY: Right. Duh. Hey.

DAISY: Hey.

APRIL: Daisy's gonna crash with us tonight, if that's cool?

LUCY: Yeah, that's no problem. I'm staying with Malcolm, anyway.

APRIL: Are you feeling okay?

LUCY: Yeah, I just haven't been sleeping well.

APRIL: Well, you know who could probably help with that?

MALCOLM: *(Off-stage)* Hello?

(APRIL *grins.* MALCOLM *enters.*)

LUCY: You disgust me.

MALCOLM: Hello?

APRIL: Speak of the devil.

MALCOLM: Yeah? What's up?

APRIL: Nothing.

LUCY: We were just objectifying you.

MALCOLM: Cool.

LUCY: I like to think so.

(*They kiss.*)

APRIL: Malcolm, this is Daisy.

MALCOLM: Nice to meet you. You guys do the thing yet?

LUCY: We're still waiting on people.

DAISY: What thing?

APRIL: This freshman girl, Sarah, she called a bunch of us like an hour ago and asked if we could meet some place where we could all talk without being interrupted, so, I volunteered here.

LUCY: Did she tell you what she wants? Cuz she wouldn't tell me anything.

APRIL: I wouldn't worry about it.

LUCY: Why not?

APRIL: Because it's Sarah Ferguson, how bad can it be?

NATALIE: (*Off-stage*) WE HAVE ARRIVED.

LUCY: Jesus Christ. Natalie?!

(NATALIE *enters with her best friend,* LIZ. LIZ *is the evening's designated driver—she's on her second cup of gas station coffee and just thrilled about it. Throughout,* LIZ *is oscillating between physically just trying to keep* NATALIE *from breaking something and having completely given up.*)

NATALIE: Sup?

LUCY: You a lil drunk?

NATALIE: (*Yep*) What? No. Why? Are you?

LUCY: No.

NATALIE: : (*Suddenly mid-interrogation*) Who did this to you? You tell me who did this to you.

APRIL: Liz?

LIZ: She wanted to get wasted, so we called Rob and Pete who have devised a game with a series of rules by which every time a rule is broken, she has to take a drink.

LUCY: Well, what are the rules?

LIZ: They won't tell anybody. But you can ask them yourself, they're outside smoking.

MALCOLM: Awesome.

NATALIE: But wait you guys wait I've gotta tell you my news.

APRIL: Wait, what?

LUCY: Natalie's got news apparently, / and if you could just?

APRIL: Really? What is it? What's the news?

LIZ: Natalie?

(NATALIE's *become distracted. Looks around*)

NATALIE: *(Beat)* Hm?

LIZ: She's going to law school.

NATALIE: You / asshole. You son of a bitch piece of shit asshole.

LUCY: What? Natalie, that's   APRIL: Congratulations,
amazing.   Natalie.

LIZ: She's very excited.

NATALIE: I was gonna tell them.

LIZ: Yeah, well, that wasn't even the best part of the news, was it? Why don't you tell them the—

NATALIE: I DON'T HAVE   LIZ: —Literally right in
TO PAY ANYTHING.   my ear.

(As the room reacts, PETE *and* ROB *enter blowing either figurative or literal party blowers. They smell like cigarettes.)*

LUCY: What? No.

LIZ: She got a call from the guy, like, two hours ago, it's this scholarship for people who want to be public defenders and it's very selective. There's gonna be a ceremony, her mother will never stop crying, but, in the meantime she's gonna get wasted.

LUCY: Well, you earned it.

APRIL: That is incredible, Nat.

PETE: Amazing, right? So cool.

ROB: And that's a drink, by the way. / Flagrant violation of the rules.

PETE: Good call.

NATALIE: *(A toast)* Drink! *(She takes a sip from a flask.)*

LUCY: And these rules you speak of?

ROB: A secret, I'm sorry to say, known only to Calvin, Peter, and myself. And not just anybody gets to play, it's an honor of sorts. Special occasions.

PETE: Bat Mitzvahs.

ROB: You want in?

LUCY: Oh, how you wish.

ROB: I do, actually.

MALCOLM: Hey, man. How ya / doin? Cool. Good talk.

ROB: Yeah.

APRIL: Rob, have you met Daisy?

ROB: Don't think so.

LUCY: From the Starbucks?

APRIL: We went to high school together. Everybody, this is Daisy. Daisy, this is everybody.

ROB: Well, I'm Rob. Welcome to our Reindeer Games.

PETE: *(Noticing)* Is Cal here?

APRIL: No, why?

PETE: I think this is his sweatshirt.

APRIL: Oh, yeah, he lent it to me last night.

ROB: Did he now?

APRIL: Stop it.

LUCY: Leave her alone.

PETE: Hey, how late were you two up last night?

LIZ: Jesus.

APRIL: Just 'til the movie ended, then he walked me back.

PETE: So, pretty late.

APRIL: So?

PETE: So, nothing. I'm just saying that would have been pretty late.

LUCY: Wait, were you two...?

LIZ: Guys.

APRIL: There's really nothing going on. Honestly. I don't know why you all...

LIZ: She's right. We're sorry.

APRIL: Look, it's gonna start snowing soon, anyway, why don't you guys just go on to Mike's and me and Liz will meet you there after?

PETE: Yeah, that sounds like a good idea—Liz, gimme your keys?

LIZ: Yeah, that's happening.

APRIL: Well, then, you'll just have to wait outside.

PETE: But it's cold outside.

APRIL: Well, Sarah didn't invite you.

PETE: Invite me for what? What are we doing here?

NATALIE: *(Taking in the space, Maria in* The Sound of Music*)* Okay, I like this. This is nice. Are we doing a play?

LIZ: No.

NATALIE: *(Re: powertools)* Are we building a house?

LIZ: Put that down.

PETE: Seriously, though, Sarah didn't say anything about…?

LIZ: Pete's freaking out.

PETE: No, he isn't.

LUCY: It is weird.

ROB: So she wouldn't say what she wanted at all?

APRIL: Just that she needed some place where we all could talk without being interrupted. That's all I know.

LUCY: Cuz that's not ominous.

PETE: And who's "we all."

APRIL: Just me, Liz, and Lucy. Oh, and Maggie.

LIZ: My sister's coming.

APRIL: Yes.

LIZ: Why is my sister coming?

APRIL: Because she's friends with Sarah? I don't know.

ROB: Drink.

*(*NATALIE *drinks.)*

LIZ: Yeah, lemme get some of that.

PETE: So she wouldn't say what she wanted to talk to you guys about? Just, hey, meet me in this creepy darkened theater in the middle of the night?

APRIL: Pretty much.

PETE: Cool, so, we're all gonna die here tonight.

MAGGIE: Hello?

(PETE *jumps as* MAGGIE *enters.)*

ROB: Oh, hey Maggie.

MAGGIE: Hey, Rob.

ROB: You here for Sarah?

LIZ: Maggie where is your coat?

ROB: I think you look nice tonight, Maggie.

MAGGIE: Thanks.

LIZ: *(Under her breath)* I hate you so much.

ROB: Me or her?

LIZ: Yes.

PETE: Maggie, you and Sarah are close, right?

MAGGIE: I mean.

PETE: Did she tell you what she wanted to talk to you guys about?

MAGGIE: I mean, if Sarah isn't here yet.

ROB: But she did tell you?

PETE: Wait, do you think it's about the party?

ROB: You mean her little.

MAGGIE: I mean.

APRIL: Guys. It's fine. If she doesn't want to say then we'll just have to wait, right? Especially those of us who were not invited in the first place?

ROB: Fine.

PETE: Cool.

APRIL: Thank you.

PETE: *(Beat)* So, what if Sarah meets us *at* the party?

(SARAH *enters in a barely-suppressed panic.*)

SARAH: Sorry I'm so sorry I'm late I was oh. Hi. Everyone. *(Beat)* Is she okay?

LIZ: She's matriculating.

SARAH: April?

APRIL: Hey, sorry, Sarah, there was kind of a miscommunication. See, Liz was already in the car with these guys when you called and Malcolm was. Well. / Sorry.

ROB: Listen, we didn't mean to crash?

PETE: Yeah, we can go if you want?

ROB: Do you want us to?

SARAH: No, I mean, you know what? Yeah, why don't we just—why don't we just do this another time?

ROB: Are you sure? / I feel bad now.

PETE: Sarah?

SARAH: Yeah?

PETE: Is everything okay?

SARAH: What? Yeah. It's fine. We'll just…

ROB: Are you sure? Because, you know, we are excellent listeners.

LIZ: They say that about you.

PETE: Seriously.

APRIL: Guys, if she doesn't / want to say, then.

SARAH: It's really not a big deal. I just—I needed some advice, and, and so I wanted to ask these guys, but.

PETE: Well, if something's wrong, I mean. I'm sure we'd all like to help, right?

ROB: Of course.

SARAH: Yeah, I just.

ROB: I mean, unless it's private? *(Re:* NATALIE*)* Cuz we can totally take Slappy over here and wait outside.

SARAH: It's not. I mean. Not really.

PETE: Is it about the party last weekend? At your parents house?

(Beat. SARAH *nods.)*

PETE: Because, you know, if you ever need help with something, anything.

ROB: Not to mention, the party was basically our idea.

LIZ: True.

PETE: So, look, if you're in some kind of trouble...

SARAH: It's not, I just. I just needed some advice, so.

PETE: So, you came to the right place, right? Right?

(Beat. SARAH *smiles. Nods)*

PETE: So, what's up?

*(*APRIL *gives her a comforting smile.* SARAH *looks around the room. Now or never)*

SARAH: Okay. Well. First of all, I mean, I really appreciate you guys coming here on a friday night, and, and with finals and the snow and everything, I, um.

(Beat. LUCY *whispers something to* MALCOLM*, who giggles.)*

SARAH: So, I found this video. See, my dad, he's got this camera, it's like, a million years old but it's got this, this really nice lens, so, so I figured maybe I should use it to take some pictures of the party last week, which, I didn't, obviously, because as you may recall I passed out pretty early.

ROB: Which was / awesome.

SARAH: Humiliating, right, and so, anyway, I passed out and then the party as you guys remember went on for a couple of hours afterwards, and I guess throughout the night, different people had it, used it, there's like, five hundred pictures and for the most part it's just the floor or people being gross, but then at the end there's this video, and I don't really know how to.

LUCY: What is it?

SARAH: A girl. *(Beat)* And she's on my kitchen table and there's a bunch of guys, they're standing around her and you can't really make out most of the faces or anything but she's on the table and she's not wearing any, um, clothes, / or anything, and there's this guy, who.

APRIL: Sarah—

LIZ: Woah woah woah wait a sec.

SARAH: And it looks like, I mean, there were a bunch of people watching, and and and yelling, and she isn't… I mean, you can't always see it quite right but at a certain point it doesn't even look like she's…

LIZ: Like she's what?

SARAH: Conscious?

APRIL: Oh, my God.

SARAH: And it also kinda looks like at a certain point, like, somebody might be holding her ankles?

LIZ: Holding her / or holding her down?

SARAH: Well, that's the thing actually.

LIZ: Holding her or holding her down?

SARAH: Well, no, that's the thing. / You can't exactly tell.

LIZ: Oh, that's the thing. And what do you mean you can't tell?

APRIL: Liz.

SARAH: I mean, I can't tell if what's going on if it's just, you know, if it's just sex on my kitchen table, which would honestly be bad enough, or if it's something else, you know. Something worse. *(Beat)* And I was gonna bring it to the cops, you know, but, but then I thought, well, what if it's nothing? What if it only looks like it's something bad but it's not but people got in trouble anyway, and?

ROB: That's smart.

SARAH: And I mean, it's not like I can show it to my parents, they don't even, and, and anybody who works at the school would just freak out, so. Look. Have any of you heard anything about this? Do any of you have any idea what I'm talking about? At all?

(Everybody looks around. Beat)

ROB: I, uh.

PETE: Sorry, Sarah.

ROB: Yeah, sorry.

MALCOLM: I wasn't even there.

DAISY: Yeah.

LIZ: I haven't heard anything.

SARAH: Nothing? *(Beat)* Well, then, I need your help.

PETE: With what?

SARAH: I mean, I found this tape and I don't know what to do with it.

PETE: So, what do you want us to do?

SARAH: Tell me what do with it.

LIZ: Okay, and this is where I jump off. / Natalie, come on. Get up. We're leaving.

SARAH: Wait a minute, what? Liz. / Where are you going?

LIZ: Natalie, get your coat. Rob, Pete, if you need a ride / either speak now…

ROB: Liz, why are you freaking out?

LIZ: I'm not freaking out. I'm just leaving right now before we do something stupid, the storm hits, and we all end up like the Donner Party. Are you coming?

ROB: Sarah asked for our help.

LIZ: Of course she did. She's terrified. Like you should be. / Natalie?

ROB: Why should I be terrified?

LIZ: Did you not hear any of what she just said? She's got a video of kids from our school, whatever, assaulting another kid from our school at a party that we all were at.

ROB: She thinks.

LIZ: Well, I don't want any part of this.

ROB: We don't even know what this is yet.

LIZ: Oh, come on.

ROB: We don't.

LIZ: Okay, look. Fine. You want me to settle this for you? Sarah, you've got this video, right? And you didn't post it any place, it isn't online? You're the only one who has it.

SARAH: Yeah.

LIZ: Then you take it to the fucking police. Because let me tell you something, if something bad did happen and the police find out that you had a tape of it and you didn't give it to them when you could have? That is when you could get into some actual, serious, real life, y'know, grown up trouble, and you don't want any part of that, okay?

SARAH: Okay.

LIZ: So, here's what you're gonna do: you're gonna go home, get some sleep, and bring that video over to the campus police or the police station with your mother first thing in the morning. In the meantime, I and my associates will head over to Mike's place so I can continue to watch Rob and Pete give my best friend alcohol poisoning. Okay?

APRIL: She's right, Sarah.

LIZ: So, we're good then?

SARAH: Yeah.

LIZ: Good.

(Everybody starts getting their shit together.)

ROB: And you guys don't think it's at all weird that we haven't heard anything about this?

APRIL: What do you mean?

ROB: I mean we go to school in the middle of nowhere with like, fifteen other kids, you don't think it's weird—

LIZ: I think people can keep a secret when they need to.

ROB: Yeah, but what people? I mean, who was it?

SARAH: In the video?

LIZ: We don't need to know that.

PETE: Are any of us / in the video?

LIZ: We don't need to know that.

SARAH: I mean, people were using the camera all night, there's tons of pictures of everybody.

PETE: But not in the video?

ROB: So, who was it?

APRIL: Who was what?

ROB: The girl? I'm just curious. I don't see what the harm is.

LIZ: I don't want to know who it was.

ROB: Why?

LIZ: For the same reason I don't want to see the video. / The less we know...

PETE: Listen, I want to know, too.

LIZ: Well, I don't.

ROB: Then cover your ears. / Who was the girl, Sarah?

LIZ: Hey.

PETE: No, not the girl. I want to know who the guy was.

ROB: Why?

PETE: So I'll know who to kick the shit out of the next time I see him.

APRIL: Pete.

PETE: I'm serious.

LIZ: And yet another reason why we shouldn't know / what's on that tape.

ROB: Well, look, Sarah asked for our help and I think before we make any sort of a decision—

LIZ: We already *made* a decision. / You aren't even supposed to be here.

ROB: *You* already made a decision.

PETE: Who was the guy, Sarah?

LIZ: Pete.

SARAH: Well, I don't know, I mean, now it seems complicated.

PETE: Complicated how?

SARAH: Well, like Liz said.

ROB: We just want to know who it was. / I mean, how are we supposed to help Sarah...?

LIZ: Well, whether you can see this or not—

SARAH: He's on the team. The guy, who. He's on the team and that's all I'm gonna say okay?

PETE: He's on the team.

SARAH: Yes.

PETE: On our / team?

SARAH: Yes.

(PETE *and* ROB *share a look; something isn't right here.*)

ROB: Look, Sarah, you did the right thing in bringing this to us. We're gonna help you figure this out, okay? Together. I promise it won't get complicated.

LIZ: Rob.

ROB: Now, who was the girl?

SARAH: Laura Heller.

Liz: Great. Well, that's just   PETE: Laura Heller?
great.

APRIL: Maggie, you're friends with Laura, right? Has she said anything about this? Should we call her?

LIZ: No, that is not what happens now. Sarah is going to bring this thing to the cops and they're gonna call her, that's their job. And the rest of us—

ROB: Well, that's assuming they do their jobs.

LIZ: Oh, come on, man.

ROB: No, look, these are small-town cops. They give parking tickets for a living. You give 'em something like this? / They'll hear rumors, see the tape, and jump to conclusions. Pete, why don't you tell 'em about Mister Webb?

LIZ: Are you serious?

PETE: Dude, I was literally / just thinking about that.

ROB: See?

APRIL: Who's Mister Webb?

PETE: Well, there was this teacher back where we went to high school, he was kind of a young guy, he was like, twenty four, right, / twenty five? We were seniors when this happened.

ROB: Twenty four, twenty five, yeah. This was in high school. And, so this kid, right, he was in the middle school?

PETE: No, he was in the high school, with us, but he posted some shit online that this teacher, Mister Webb, that he'd, like, done something or whatever with one of the girls in the middle school.

LIZ: Look.

ROB: Within like, three days, there was this petition.

PETE: Three hundred something names on it.

ROB: No joke.

PETE: Students, parents, other teachers, even.

ROB: A couple of cops, too, actually, which is fucked / if you think about it.

PETE: Right. They all sign this petition to get him fired.

ROB: So, what happens? The next day after, he is fired. The next day after that, he gets arrested.

PETE: It was insane.

ROB: Guy goes on trial where they find literally zero evidence of anything, he doesn't go to jail, but still all anyone can think of is maybe he *did* do something and got away with it.

PETE: Right, and so now this guy who did nothing wrong.

ROB: Nobody'll talk to him, nobody'll hire him.

PETE: Right, and by the end of it his whole life is just so entirely fucked, that he. Y'know.

MALCOLM: What?

ROB: He put a gun in his mouth. Guy was twenty-five years old and he put a gun in his mouth because people started spreading rumors when they should have just minded their own goddam business.

LIZ: And I get that, I hear what you are saying, but guess what? This isn't a post online. This is a video in Sarah's bag that I'm sorry, I am just not going to make a part of my life. So, you guys do whatever you feel like you need to do. Sarah, you bring that thing to the cops / like we talked about and everything will be fine, okay? I'm outta here.

ROB: No. That's not—no. Liz. Listen to me, would you just—hey. (*Grabbing* SARAH's *bag*) She is not bringing it to the cops until we've agreed. / All of us. And you're not leaving. You can't.

MALCOLM: Sorry, what? Why?

LIZ: Excuse me?

ROB: Look, I'm sorry.

LIZ: What is going on here?

ROB: I just think we all need to be on the same page.

LIZ: You are literally the only person here who's not on the same page about this. / Now, get out of my way.

PETE: No, he isn't.

LIZ: Pete.

APRIL: Rob, how are you so sure?

ROB: I didn't say I was sure, I said I wasn't convinced.

LIZ: You want me to go through you?

PETE: Put the bag down, man. Just relax.

(ROB *gives the bag to* PETE, *who hands it back to* SARAH.)

ROB: Look, I'm sorry, I just, if it was anybody else I'd say fine, sure, maybe something bad happened but Laura Heller and a guy on the team? / Pete? Come on.

DAISY: Who's Laura Heller?

LIZ: Rob.

ROB: No, look, you said I was the only one, right? Pete. Come on. Back me up on this.

PETE: On what?

DAISY: Who's Laura Heller?

APRIL: She's a sophomore.

ROB: A sophomore who, look, I'm not saying anything bad or anything, just, you know, she's always been a little, what?

PETE: Obsessive.

ROB: Yes. Exactly.

DAISY: Obsessed with what?

PETE: I mean.

ROB: With us.

APRIL: With you and Pete?

PETE: And Cal and Marshall and Wallace.

ROB: Mike Watts.

PETE: Mike Watts, Matt Lazarus.

ROB: Seth Kannof, and basically every other guy on the lacrosse team and it's not, look, she came to literally every single lacrosse game last year, did you know that? I didn't even go to every lacrosse game last year and I'm *on* the lacrosse team.

APRIL: So did I.

ROB: Well, exactly, because we're friends, you're friends with us, which she isn't. But she's always there, and she's always, like, texting.

PETE: It's true, no, do you want to see how many messages I have from her?

LIZ: What's your point?

PETE: I'm still scrolling.

ROB: And, look, do you guys remember what she was wearing that night?

(The room reacts.)

APRIL: Are you serious?   LUCY: That's disgusting.

ROB: Look, I know what you guys, look, okay, so here this is what Laura was wearing—I'm on her profile by the way—and this is what Laura was wearing, now that's not even—that's not even a dress, okay, that is a skirt, which happens to, it's a tanktop, basically, and she's wearing it as a skirt. Now are you telling me --?

LUCY: That doesn't mean anything.

ROB: Of course it does, why else does your boyfriend look like he's dressed for picture day in the fourth grade? No offense.

MALCOLM: None taken.

ROB: He got dressed up. For you. Like you got dressed up for him. It's why April got all dressed up to go see Cal at the party. (I'm sorry. But it's adorable.) And it's not a bad thing. It's just what people do.

APRIL: So?

ROB: So, Laura Heller comes to a party dressed like that and ends up having sex with some guy she's crazy about anyway, which is historically, everyone? Seriously. How is that weird?

APRIL: On a table? With somebody filming it? You don't think that's weird?

ROB: I think it was a weird night. Look, do you remember what Sarah got up to that night? And this is Sarah Ferguson we're talking about, here.

SARAH: We could also not, actually.

ROB: Look.

MALCOLM: Wait, what happened?

ROB: There was a kind of a, what's the word?

PETE: A dance.

ROB: There was a kind of a dance that was done. / Thank you, Pete.

APRIL: Guys, we are not gonna talk about this.

LIZ: We shouldn't be talking about any of this.

PETE: It was a sort of a.

ROB: A strip tease? / Is that the word?

PETE: I'm pretty sure that's, yeah. The technical term.

SARAH: I don't remember this at all. I swear.

ROB: I do.

MAGGIE: I do, too, actually.

MALCOLM: Really?

MAGGIE: It was pretty rad, actually.

APRIL: Guys.

SARAH: You saw it?

MAGGIE: I got it.

PETE: It was a kind of a lap-dance, at points.

MALCOLM: Really.

APRIL: Guys, it was not that serious. She tripped over her own shoelace trying to get her sock off and me and Lucy put her to bed around ten.

SARAH: And how did we get to talking about this?

ROB: Because *this* is Exhibit B, okay? This is proof that weird, public, sometimes even sexual shit happens at parties like this all the time and while it may seem weird now, in the context.

PETE: Totally normal.

ROB: Exactly, and so since we don't know the context of whatever's on that tape, but considering the chaos and damage that could ensue if we bring it to the local, whatever, sheriff's office, I think the most responsible thing that we can do is to just forget about it.

DAISY: So, why don't we just watch it? *(Beat)* Sorry, did I miss the part where that's not obvious?

LUCY: The video?

LIZ: No. Absolutely not. / No.

DAISY: Why?

LIZ: You know exactly why.

DAISY: I don't, actually.

PETE: Liz.

LIZ: Because we're involved, then. / If we watch it—

DAISY: We're not involved yet?

LIZ: It's different. / It would be different.

DAISY: How?

LIZ: Because we haven't actually seen anything yet. We've still got, whatever, we haven't actually seen anything and as far as we know.

DAISY: Well, yeah, but—

LIZ: We watch it and its a whole other thing. Trust me.

DAISY: Well, yeah, but nothing else that you're saying makes any sense.

ROB: What do you mean?

DAISY: I mean you said that she came to the party dressed like a slut / and that she's got a hard on for these guys on your team, right? But at the start of all this, that one said it looked like she might be unconscious, right?

ROB: Which, those are your words, by the way. Not mine.

SARAH: Yeah?

DAISY: Well, if she was unconscious then none of the rest of this matters. If she's unconscious, you stop fucking her. Period. The end. Is this not very obvious to everyone else?

APRIL: She's right.

DAISY: So, we watch the video and if she's asleep we take it to the cops. That's it.

ROB: Well, sure, except Sarah already watched the video and she couldn't tell what was going on.

DAISY: Well, maybe we'll see something that she didn't. / I mean, unless you've got something to hide—

LIZ: It's a bad idea, Daisy.

PETE: Excuse me?

DAISY: What?

PETE: What did you just say?

APRIL: Pete.

PETE: No, what did she just say?

DAISY: I said unless you've got something to hide. Unless he's got—

PETE: Like what?

ROB: Pete, it's fine.

PETE: No, it is not fine. / It's not fine. She can't just—

DAISY: What, look, this guy's been having, like, heart palpitations since Sarah first brought it up. We're all just supposed to what? Not notice?

APRIL: Daisy.

DAISY: No, come on, he's the only one who doesn't want to watch this thing and I'm wondering why.

LIZ: He isn't, actually.

DAISY: Right, which, your O C D about it is totally normal, by the way. / There's either something you don't want to see or something you don't want us to see but one way or the other—

ROB: You know what, here, I'm standing right here, you want to ask me something, Daisy? / Ask me the question. Ask the question.

APRIL: Of course she doesn't, right, Daisy?

DAISY: If we watch that thing, are we gonna see you on top of her?

PETE: See, that's not okay.

DAISY: He asked.

PETE: You can't just. / That's not okay.

DAISY: He told me to ask the question / which he still hasn't answered.

PETE: How could you even think, for a second that—

DAISY: Look, I don't know you people.

PETE: No, you don't, because if you did you wouldn't ask that. I've known this guy my entire life. He wouldn't ever—not ever do anything remotely like that. That's not who he is.

DAISY: He still hasn't answered my question.

PETE: Because he doesn't have to.

DAISY: Why?

PETE: Because we don't know you. This is my best friend, okay?

DAISY: So, was it you, then?

PETE: You know what?

ROB: Dude. It's okay.

PETE: No, it is not okay. / It's not.

ROB: Look, I can settle this right now, okay. Sarah. Was I in the video?

PETE: Dude.

ROB: Was I?

SARAH: No. You. He wasn't. I swear.

ROB: Was Pete?

SARAH: No. Neither of them were.

ROB: Okay?

PETE: Nice friend you got here, April.

DAISY: Fine. I'm sorry.

APRIL: Pete, she doesn't know you guys, okay?

PETE: No, she doesn't.

DAISY: I'm sorry, okay? Jesus.

APRIL: She doesn't know you guys, what would you think?

PETE: Maybe I would listen.

LIZ: We really shouldn't be talking about this.

ROB: All right, can I just say something without everybody jumping down my throat?

PETE: Best of luck.

ROB: Because I'm just, you know, I'm just trying to think all this through, logically, and I'm thinking about—does anybody else remember how last year, how Laura used to post all that stuff about her parents getting divorced? Does anybody else remember that? It was like, stuff about her dad, conversations, with like, how she was seeing a psychiatrist, right?

PETE: Yeah.

ROB: All this really sad stuff, depression and anxiety and stuff, to like this weird level of detail.

APRIL: So?

ROB: So if Laura Heller got hurt like we hope she didn't, do you really think that she would keep that to herself? I mean, honestly, don't you think she would have said something?

SARAH: Well, actually, she probably wouldn't even have had to.

ROB: Had to what?

SARAH: Tell anybody. I mean, when you get attacked, you've gotta go to the hospital, / there's all this stuff, that, and if she did go to the hospital, like she woulda had to...

DAISY: What are you talking about?

ROB: Exactly, right, so if something happened then she would have had to have gone to the hospital, at which point the hospital would have had to have called the police, at which point the police would have swarmed the school.

PETE: Which they haven't, ergo nothing happened.

ROB: Exactly.

NATALIE: You don't have to go to the hospital. *(Beat)* What?

DAISY: You were saying something?

NATALIE: I, uh.

ROB: Does she need to lie down?

APRIL: Natalie? What were you going to say?

NATALIE: Well, I knew a girl this one time who was coming home one night...

LIZ: Natalie, maybe...

NATALIE: She was coming home from a bar and, she'd never been to a bar before and, because she was younger than they were, her friends insisted she took a cab home, because they wanted her to be safe, you know, and so she got to her door and the cab drove away, and at some point in between opening the door and closing the door and the cab driving away, while she was getting the key out for the, um. There was. *(Beat)* Anyway, she had this thing happen, where, you know there's this wall on the inside it's a very important wall and when it gets hurt, there's. And there's blood everywhere, sometimes, you know. But. Um. *(Beat)* But you know, you don't have to go to the hospital right away if you don't want to. You just got the shit kicked out of you. You don't have to do anything if you don't want to. If you want, you can just sit there. Bleed for a bit, if you're bleeding. Or if you want you can go to the hospital and you can give a fake name or a fake insurance and then when they're not looking, you can go, but, you don't have to go right away. Not if you don't want to. *(Beat)* She hasn't even told her mom yet. *(Beat)* What was I saying?

ROB: All right, look—

LUCY: Maybe we should take a vote.

LIZ: A vote?

MALCOLM: Like a preliminary, right?

PETE: Why?

MALCOLM: So we can see where we are.

LIZ: I'm not sure that's such a good idea.

LUCY: Why?

DAISY: She doesn't want to get involved. That's just an educated guess.

LIZ: I just don't see the need, is all.

LUCY: But we keep going around in circles about this and besides, I think it's important everybody's voice is heard, and honestly, it can be difficult to get a word in.

MALCOLM: That's not a bad point.

LIZ: Lucy.

LUCY: All right, so how about this then: Liz, everybody, you wanna get out of here, right? So, how about this: if we vote and if Rob, or, if Rob and Pete are the only ones who think it's a bad idea and the rest of us vote otherwise, then they'll step aside and Sarah takes it to the cops. Right?

MALCOLM: Makes sense to me.

LUCY: Rob?

ROB: Works for me. Liz?

LIZ: Fine.

LUCY: Sarah, why don't you do the honors, okay?

SARAH: Okay.

APRIL: Maybe we should close our eyes?

ROB: Why?

APRIL: I think people might have an easier time being honest if they close their eyes.

ROB: That's smart.

APRIL: Thanks.

SARAH: Okay. So, um. I'll do yes, no, or abstention. Okay? Okay. Everybody close your eyes. All in favor of taking it to the cops?

(APRIL, DAISY, LIZ, LUCY, MALCOLM, *and* NATALIE *all raise their hands.*)

SARAH: All opposed?

(PETE, ROB, *and, after a moment,* MAGGIE *raise their hands.*)

SARAH: Um. Abstentions? *(She raises her hand.)* Okay, it's, uh. Six to three in favor of taking it to the cops. And one abstention.

PETE: So, who was the third? On our side?

ROB: Liz?

LIZ: Seriously?

ROB: *(Re:* NATALIE*)* What about this one?

SARAH: She voted yes, too.

DAISY: Don't look at me.

APRIL: Or me.

LUCY: I'm with them.

MALCOLM: Yeah, me too.

SARAH: I abstained.

ROB: So, wait, so that means.

PETE: No. Fucking. Way.

(They all turn to see MAGGIE, *who does her best to look casual.)*

LIZ: Maggie?

ROB: She doesn't have to explain herself.

LIZ: I think she does.

MAGGIE: It wasn't what you guys think, okay?

LIZ: What does that mean?

APRIL: Liz.

LIZ: No, what do you mean? Did Laura say something to you about this?

MAGGIE: No.

LIZ: Then I don't understand, what are you—

DAISY: Wait, were you in the room? With Laura? When this happened?

MAGGIE: I mean.

LIZ: Answer the question, please.

MAGGIE: *(Beat)* Yes, I was. / Yes. But it wasn't.

LIZ: Fucking shit.

DAISY: So, what happened?

APRIL: Maggie, why didn't you say anything about this this whole time?

ROB: She was probably just scared. / Would you lay off her?

APRIL: Scared of what? Of us?

DAISY: What happened?

MAGGIE: Nothing happened.

APRIL: Maggie.

MAGGIE: Nothing happened. It was, look, it was weird, okay? Or not weird, it was, I mean, it was late. There were these Christmas tree lights all strung up, so it was all red and green and soft.

APRIL: Maggie, listen—

MAGGIE: It was beautiful. And we had all sorta split off, two by two, we had all been drinking, and, you know and everybody sorta started—

(MAGGIE *sees the look on* LIZ's *face*.)

MAGGIE: But then people started laughing, you know, cheering, and, because, because they saw what they were doing and so we went to go and look and.

DAISY: And you just watched?

MAGGIE: We all did. It wasn't—it's so hard to explain it, you know? Because it wasn't like—

DAISY: What?

MAGGIE: Scary. It wasn't scary and it wasn't violent. It was—beautiful. I mean, they were lying down on, or, well, technically, *she* was lying down on the island in your kitchen, Sarah, like you said, and I just remember thinking, you know, I don't think I've ever seen Laura look so happy before. I mean, he was kissing her, you know. *He* was kissing *her*. Nobody kisses Laura Heller like that. Nobody. And I know what you think of her and believe me, she does, too. But she's not, you know, she's not a bad person, she just, she just tries too hard sometimes, because she wants so bad for somebody to like her. To pay attention to her. Like that.

APRIL: Maggie.

MAGGIE: And so when I saw her, and he was, you know, he was holding her and kissing her and everything, I mean, I knew it was strange, but after what Sarah had done earlier, I thought, well, maybe it's not, you know? Maybe this is just what happens. And nobody else seemed to find it weird, and they didn't even seem to notice, but, and I know you think she's like this big attention whore and everything but if this video got out and people saw? She would hate that. Seriously. Like, if she even knew that you guys had a tape or that you were talking about her like this? She would hate that. She would lose it. Seriously. So, yeah, if you want my opinion, then, yeah, I think it would be a really bad idea to take this thing to the police. I think Rob was right, you know? I think this might have been the best night of her life. I mean. It was the best night of mine.

DAISY: They didn't notice?

MAGGIE: What?

DAISY: You said they didn't seem to notice, when you were—

MAGGIE: Yeah.

DAISY: Were her eyes open?

MAGGIE: What do you mean?

DAISY: Her eyes. Were they open?

MAGGIE: I mean, they were kissing, and—I don't understand.

APRIL: Sarah said she looked like she might be unconscious, Maggie. Was she?

MAGGIE: Of course she wasn't. I mean, she was. She wasn't unconscious.

DAISY: So, her eyes were open and everything?

MAGGIE: I mean, they were kissing, so. / Look, we wouldn't have let something like that happen.

DAISY: What does that mean?

PETE: Daisy, maybe you wanna relax?

DAISY: No, what does that mean, / 'they were kissing.'

MAGGIE: It means that sometimes when people are kissing they close their eyes.

DAISY: So, her eyes were closed, then. Was she moving?

MAGGIE: Wait, that's.

DAISY: Was she?

MAGGIE: Yes. Of course.

ROB: Jesus, Daisy.

DAISY: Okay, like, what, what was she doing?

ROB: Daisy, this isn't—   PETE: I don't want to hear
                                  about this.

DAISY: What were her hands doing?

ROB: Are you getting off on this?

APRIL: Rob.

DAISY: What were her hands doing?

MAGGIE: What do you mean?

DAISY: Was she touching him with her hands, was she
kissing him?

MAGGIE: I can't remember.

DAISY: You can't remember?

MAGGIE: I mean, no, I do. Of course, I do, I just—

DAISY: So, was she holding him, this guy, whoever this
mystery guy / might be, was she touching him?

PETE: Daisy.

DAISY: Was she kissing him? Was she moving at all?

MAGGIE: I don't—no.

DAISY: Then how do you know that she wasn't
unconscious? (Beat) Maggie?

MAGGIE: Liz?

DAISY: Okay, then, that's it. / We're taking it to the
cops.

APRIL: She's right.

MAGGIE: Wait. I don't understand. Why—what did I
say?

ROB: *(He gets in* DAISY's *way)* All right, / hang on.

MAGGIE: What did I say? / Lizzie?

DAISY: No, it's done. There isn't any question anymore. She was unconscious. That was what Sarah didn't know and now we know.

ROB: What? Because she said she was? She was drunk. She said she was drunk.

DAISY: Gimme the tape, Sarah. / You asked us for our help, you said you wanted to do the right thing, didn't you? Didn't you?

ROB: Sarah, do not give here that tape. Are you listening to me or not? Daisy.

SARAH: Yes.

DAISY: Then give me your dad's / fucking camera.

ROB: We haven't even made / a decision yet.

DAISY: You guys need more evidence? Great. Let's bring it to the cops and I'm sure they'll find us some. / But we know what happened now.

MAGGIE: Lizzie? Liz, you've gotta tell them. It's not—

PETE: There's a lot on the line, here, Daisy, we just want to be sure before we risk / turning somebody's life upside down.

DAISY: Just give it to me, okay? Give it to me and it won't be on your shoulders anymore.

ROB: And we said we were all / gonna have to agree before.

DAISY: You said that. I never said anything.

ROB: We all need to be on / the same page about this.

DAISY: Well, what is it going to take for us all to be on the same page?

MAGGIE: Lizzie, please.

LIZ: *(Breaks something)* Maggie, would you just shut the fuck up?!

(Beat. Everybody's watching.)

LIZ: We're not bringing it to the cops.

DAISY: Excuse me?

LIZ: We aren't having this discussion anymore, Daisy. April, please, don't fight me on this. We aren't releasing that tape. Now, / this thing happened...

DAISY: Oh, really.

LIZ: This thing happened and now it's over and it's too late for us to do anything about it, too late for the cops to do anything about it, run any tests. / It's been six days.

DAISY: Are you serious?

APRIL: Liz, not twenty minutes ago you looked at / Sarah and you said—

LIZ: And I was wrong, then. / I was wrong.

APRIL: Because you didn't know Maggie was there?

LIZ: Because it isn't going to do anything. It isn't going to help anybody. All it's gonna do is hurt the wrong people and I'm not / gonna let that happen.

DAISY: Hurt the wrong people, like who, like Maggie? You aren't worried about Laura, obviously.

LIZ: No, I am worried about Laura, but I am also worried about Sarah, and Maggie and Natalie and Lucy and Pete. / I'm worried about all of us.

APRIL: What are you talking about?

LIZ: I'm talking about what do you think happens to Sarah when her parents find out that she threw a party at their house where a girl got assaulted on their kitchen table? Lucy, you're applying to med-schools next year, do you really want this hanging around your neck? Malcolm, how do you think that's gonna go for her? "Say, didn't you go to the rape school? Weren't you at that party" How does John's Hopkins usually feel about that sort of thing?

MAGGIE: That isn't what happened. That isn't what happened, Liz.

LIZ: Yes. It. Is. *(Beat)* It just doesn't matter.

APRIL: Liz.

LIZ: What about law school, Nat? What would your mom think? This, this would break her heart, do you realize that? After she worked so hard to get you here, after everything. If she found out that you were at a party like this? If they took away your scholarship? Do you really think they're gonna want you anymore, Natalie?

DAISY: You are so full of shit.

LIZ: No, I'm not. The media and the fucking, whatever, people online, they will show our pictures, day after day after day and they will blame us for being there and letting this happen.

APRIL: That's not what happened.

LIZ: Well, it doesn't matter what happened. It matters what it looks like. Now, you tell me, okay? How does this look for us, if we become associated with this?

DAISY: That's not good enough.

ROB: *(Pissed)* Well, not for you, maybe. But why would it be?

APRIL: Rob.

ROB: No, true or false, Daisy, this time next year you're gonna be working at the Dunkin Donuts / or whatever anyway so what do you care if—

APRIL: Don't you / talk to her like that. Don't you dare talk to her like that.

ROB: With your holier than thou bullshit, ya fuckin' townie. Like what?

APRIL: Like you're better than her.

PETE: Do we all want to take a breather, here?

LIZ: This is all beside the point.

APRIL: So what is the point?

LIZ: This isn't our responsibility.

LUCY: Yes, it is.

LIZ: Why?

LUCY: Because we're the only ones with the tape.

DAISY: Yes. Thank you.

LUCY: She didn't tell anyone, she didn't go to the hospital.

MALCOLM: She's right.

LUCY: She didn't call the cops—she could have no idea what's happening to her.

LIZ: Which would be a bad thing? Lucy, if by some miracle, she doesn't remember what happened to her then who in the hell are we to remind her of that? What possible good would that do?

LUCY: Because she could be sick. She could be sick and scared and alone, she could be pregnant, and we might just be the only ones who know about it, if it isn't our responsibility—

LIZ: She's my sister. She's in the video. I don't have a choice.

APRIL: (Getting her phone out) Yeah, and neither did Laura, apparently. But I do. I do have a choice, and I'm gonna do what we should have done an hour ago. I'm gonna call her.

ROB: April, you don't / want to do that.

LIZ: April, just stop. Just think for a second and wait.

APRIL: Wait for what? She's been living with this for six days.

ROB: And we've had it for less than an hour.

PETE: Okay, maybe we should all / just calm down.

APRIL: No, I need to talk to her, I need to talk to her and make sure that she's okay. Maggie, give me your phone.

LIZ: Maggie, do not—

ROB: April.

APRIL: Maggie, give me your phone. Please.

LIZ: Maggie.

APRIL: Sarah, please. / I just need her number. Maggie?

ROB: April, you call her right now and you are only gonna make this thing ten times more complicated. / You're gonna turn this whole thing into...

APRIL: I need to know if she's okay. / That is the only thing that matters.

ROB: April, you do this and you'll regret it.

DAISY: Was that a threat?

ROB: This isn't what you think it was. / None of it.

APRIL: So, what was it, then?

(DAISY *snags* MAGGIE's *phone and hands it to* APRIL.)

MAGGIE: Hey!

LIZ: What the fuck?

ROB: Are you a child?

APRIL: I'm calling her.

LIZ: Put the phone down, April.

DAISY: Back off.

LIZ: Do you wanna get out of my face, please?

ROB: April, please. You don't want to do this.

APRIL: Why?

ROB: You just—

APRIL: No, I need a reason. / Not hypothetical, not—

ROB: You just have to trust me.

APRIL: That's not good enough.

ROB: April, stop.

APRIL: Why?

ROB: Because it's Cal.

(Beat)

LAURA: *(O S. Filtered)* Hello? Hello? Is anybody—

(APRIL hangs up. Beat)

ROB: Y'see? I told you, didn't I? Didn't I tell you? I told you to just trust me if you'd just trusted me.

PETE: How did you know that?

ROB: Pete.

PETE: Were you in the room?

SARAH: You weren't. / I never saw you there.

ROB: Listen to me, everybody listen to me right now.

SARAH: I didn't see you in the video.

PETE: Were you in the room?

LIZ: You were there?

ROB: Listen, I never lied to you.

PETE: Robbie? *(His face is a mask of disbelief and horror.)*

ROB: Look, I was drunk. We all were. But it wasn't—

PETE: Was she unconscious?

ROB: Pete. / It wasn't what you think.

SARAH: I didn't see you in the room.

LIZ: What are you talking about?

PETE: Was she unconscious?

ROB: Pete.

PETE: Was she?

ROB: It was like what Maggie said, okay? People started getting sloppy. Everybody was making out, Cal and Laura, they just took it further than the rest of us. It's not like he's some guy in an alley. It's Cal. Cal wouldn't do that. And I didn't lie about anything. I just wanted to keep his name out of it in case stuff got, you know...

PETE: Sloppy?

ROB: Yes. Yes, exactly. But I never lied to you. I was gonna tell you the second we left, all of it, I swear. I just didn't think it was important. You get that, right?

DAISY: Wait, so, which was it?

ROB: What do you mean?

DAISY: Were you gonna tell him after / or did you not think it was important?

ROB: You want to stay out of this, please?

DAISY: And after you made us sit through all that bullshit about what clothes she was wearing, if she wanted it, / this was about you saving your own ass?

ROB: Listen, would you just listen?

SARAH: You're not on the tape.

ROB: What?

DAISY: What are you talking about?

SARAH: You aren't on the tape, Rob, you're not in the / video. How can you— Oh.

ROB: What does it matter whether—

SARAH: Oh. Right.

APRIL: What?

SARAH: You filmed it. Right?

LIZ: You filmed it?

ROB: I mean.

LIZ: Idiot.

PETE: Robbie.

DAISY: You don't disappoint, Rob, / I'll give you that.

ROB: Would you shut the fuck up?

LIZ: You stupid fucking idiot child / do you understand what you've done?

ROB: Liz.

PETE: Why would you film it?

ROB: I thought it'd be funny. *(Beat)* I mean, Cal Summers and Laura Heller? I thought. *(Beat)* Look, it was a mistake. It's Cal, you guys. You know Cal. He's our friend. And I'm serious, now.

DAISY: This is pathetic.

ROB: *(Getting worked up, a little desperate)* It was a mistake. He's not like, it's not like he's the guy who hurt Natalie. This is different than that. What that was was terrible but this, this is just two people—he just made a mistake. He's a kid. The night was crazy but he's just a kid, like we all are, he's got his whole life ahead of him, and. Do you guys really believe that he deserves to have his whole life thrown away? Because of one night? One mistake, with a girl who was crazy about him anyway?

APRIL: Shut up.

ROB: April.

APRIL: Just shut up.

ROB: April, please.

DAISY: She said—

APRIL: He's right.

DAISY: *(Beat)* April?

APRIL: There has to be something we don't know.

DAISY: What are you / talking about?

APRIL: Cal wouldn't do this. I'm sorry, Daisy, but he wouldn't. / There's just no way.

DAISY: He was drunk.

APRIL: Yeah, well I've seen Cal drunk. He isn't like that.

PETE: He can be.

APRIL: Not with me.

DAISY: He wasn't with you.

APRIL: He wouldn't do this.

DAISY: You don't know that.

APRIL: I know him.

DAISY: April.

APRIL: It's Cal. I mean, do you have any idea, Daisy, look at me, do you have any idea how many times he's walked me back late at night and / there has to be something…

DAISY: I can't believe I'm hearing this.

APRIL: And last night, we were on his couch and nobody else was there and then we went for a walk, all alone, I was gone, and if he wanted to. But he didn't. He didn't because he wouldn't. Not ever.

DAISY: April.

APRIL: No, there's gotta be something else that we don't know. Maggie and Rob said they were flirting, maybe? Maybe they talked about it before. Maybe she wanted to, and.

DAISY: April, listen to me.

APRIL: He wouldn't hurt anyone.

DAISY: You don't know that.

APRIL: I know him. He's my friend.

DAISY: And if it was me?

APRIL: If it was you, then I would stand by you, too, / I wouldn't—

DAISY: I mean if it was me instead of Laura.

APRIL: That isn't—

ROB: He just made a mistake. / They both did.

DAISY: And who's to say he won't make it again?

APRIL: He won't. / He wouldn't. He didn't.

DAISY: But you don't know that. You don't know that, April.

APRIL: Daisy, I know Cal like you know me.

DAISY: I don't know you.

(Beat. This hits APRIL *like a shot.)*

NATALIE: What if we just wait? Is that… could we do that?

PETE: Wait for what?

NATALIE: For us to get out of here, graduate. Get jobs or our lives set up. I mean, couldn't we just… wait? Why does it have to… I just don't get why it has to be now? That doesn't seem fair.

DAISY: Fair to who?

ROB: We need to make a decision. Tonight.

SARAH: Then maybe we should vote again? Might be good to see where we're at.

LIZ: Vote for what?

SARAH: Well, I figure we all need to—I mean, if we don't all agree, then.

ROB: She's right.

SARAH: I mean, even if it's just one of us, anybody could.

PETE: Yeah, okay.

SARAH: So it'll be unanimous. Whatever we agree?

APRIL: Eyes closed?

DAISY: Our eyes should be open this time.

APRIL: Why?

DAISY: Because our eyes should be open this time.

APRIL: Fine.

SARAH: All in favor of bringing the tape to the cops?

(DAISY, LUCY, *and* MALCOLM *raise their hands.*)

SARAH: All opposed?

(APRIL, LIZ, MAGGIE, NATALIE, PETE, *and* ROB *raise their hands. Six to three*)

SARAH: Abstentions?

ROB: Time to pick a side, Sarah.

(SARAH *raises her hand.*)

SARAH: Seven to three.

DAISY: Well, that wasn't so hard, was it?

NATALIE: I wanna go home.

ROB: We're almost there.

NATALIE: Drink.

(NATALIE *takes her flask out and starts drinking again. She finishes it.* LIZ *just looks away.*)

DAISY: I really don't know what you guys are expecting to, we know what happened now, do you guys get that? There isn't any mystery anymore. We *know* what happened.

APRIL: No, we don't.

(APRIL's *phone rings.*)

DAISY: Who's that?

(APRIL *silences her phone.*)

ROB: Lucy, I get that you're pissed at me, but this is Cal we're talking about. He could go to jail, do you get that? Prison. For nothing.

LUCY: I don't care.

ROB: You should.

LIZ: Well, what about Laura?

DAISY: What about Laura?

LIZ: I mean, it's been a week. If she hasn't said anything, / which she hasn't—

DAISY: Assuming she knows what happened in the first place.

LIZ: Which she hasn't, isn't that her telling us what she wants? By not saying anything? Maybe she doesn't want people knowing. I mean I wouldn't want this out there, if it was me? I mean, think about it, we bring this thing to the cops? And it leaks, because of course it will? That video, that picture of her, that'll live online. Forever. This would define / her for the rest of her life. People would be calling her house, she'd get death threats.

DAISY: Do you actually believe any of this bullshit you're saying?

ROB: You know, Daisy, we've got a responsibility to protect her, too, you know.

MALCOLM: You are so full of shit, Rob.

ROB: Hang on. Has he been here this whole time?

MALCOLM: No, come on, this isn't for her. You're not doing / this for her. This is about you.

ROB: The fuck are you talking about?

MALCOLM: I mean, I've been sitting here, watching you guys fall all over yourselves trying to come up with something that sounds better than "I don't give a shit". I mean, come on. "It was a mistake"? Locking your keys in the car is a mistake. This was rape. Oh, that's right, I'm sorry, we're not supposed to say that word, are we? Well that's what it is.

DAISY: Where the fuck have you been?

ROB: That is not what it is. / You weren't there. You don't know what the fuck you're talking about.

MALCOLM: He had sex with a girl who drank too much and fell asleep what in the hell else would you call that?

ROB: And they were both drunk, okay? They were both drunk. / And you weren't even…

MALCOLM: So, what?

ROB: So, why are we holding him to a higher standard when they were both drunk?

MALCOLM: Because it's different.

ROB: How?

MALCOLM: Because he could stand.

LUCY: He's right.

MALCOLM: You know, you keep trying to make this seem more complicated than it is but it isn't complicated, Rob. He made a choice. And so did you. And so did you, April. This isn't about her. You want to screw this girl? The least you could do is be honest about it.

ROB: You know, I think I liked you better when you didn't talk.

APRIL: Malcolm.

MALCOLM: Well, you can keep talking all you want, Rob, but I'm done listening. I am taking that camera to the cops and I am going to tell them what happened here and if you destroy it or if they don't believe me then I am going to post about it online all day every day until somebody does. This is wrong. It's just black and it's white and it's wrong.

LIZ: Says the only guy who wasn't at the party.

MALCOLM: Meaning what?

LIZ: Meaning you've got a shit-ton less to lose than the rest of us.

ROB: Oh, I wouldn't say that.

MALCOLM: Really? I would. Because guess what, I'm not like everybody else in this room: I'm not your friend, I'm not Cal's friend, I'm not Maggie's sister, and I'm not on that fucking video.

ROB: She is. *(He's pointing right at* LUCY.*)*

MALCOLM: Fuck you.

ROB: I'm sorry about this, Luce.

MALCOLM: No, she isn't.

ROB: It's not like it / wasn't gonna get out anyway.

LUCY: Malcolm.

MALCOLM: Are you listening to me? Hey. I said, / no, she isn't.

ROB: Then why don't you ask her, then?

MALCOLM: Because I don't have to ask her.

ROB: Why?

MALCOLM: Because I know her.

LUCY: Malcolm. *(Beat)* Look, can we just talk about this outside?

MALCOLM: You were there?

LUCY: Look.

ROB: Huh.

MALCOLM: I don't understand. / You were there?

ROB: That's weird.

LUCY: Malcolm, please, why don't we just—

MALCOLM: And you didn't tell me?

ROB: I wonder what else she hasn't told you.

*(*MALCOLM *lunges for* ROB. *They wrestle for a moment until the group splits them up.)*

LUCY: Stop it.

*(*PETE *puts* ROB *into a wall and pins him there, anger coursing through him. Beat. After a moment,* PETE *lets go and walks away.)*

ROB: *(To* MALCOLM*)* Psycho.

LUCY: Mal.

MALCOLM: Well, I guess that's it, then, right? All in favor?

LUCY: What are you—no, wait, / what are you—what are you talking about?

MALCOLM: Now I've gotta do this too, right? / Now, I've gotta—

LUCY: No, look, listen to me. I can explain.

MALCOLM: What do you have to explain?

LUCY: Malcolm.

MALCOLM: You were there, weren't you?

LUCY: Which is why—

MALCOLM: Then what do you have to explain?!

LUCY: I have to make this right.

LIZ: It isn't going to make it right, Lucy.

LUCY: Look, I fucked up, you think I don't know I fucked up? *(Re: her head)* Do you wanna know it's like up here? Yes, I was there. Yes, I knew what was happening. And I could have stopped it, I just. I got scared. I froze. I fucked up. And I have had to live with that, but this—

LIZ: Lucy, listen to me.

LUCY: This is my chance to fix this. This is all happening for a reason. So we can bring it to the cops. So I can make it right.

LIZ: But it isn't going to make it right.

LUCY: Liz.

LIZ: No, it isn't going to make it right. It is only going to hurt a lot of other people. / And to what? Make you feel better?

LUCY: It's the right thing to do, Liz. You know that.

LIZ: I don't know that.

LUCY: I have to do this.

LIZ: Then why didn't you just do it already? No, I mean it. You've had six days of feeling terrible, why didn't you just say something?

LUCY: I was scared.

LIZ: No, it's not because you were scared, it's because you knew, deep down, that while maybe it would feel like it was the right thing to do…

LUCY: Liz.

LIZ: …And maybe it would make you feel better, it would only end up getting a lot of other people hurt. People who didn't do anything wrong. And you know something else, Lucy? You were right.

LUCY: No, I'm sorry, but I can't—I have to—

LIZ: Bringing it to the cops won't undo what happened, it won't help Laura and it won't change what you or Rob or anybody else did. What it will do is hurt every single person in this room. Everyone. And I know that you want to do the right thing, here, but Lucy, you and me, together, we can do the right thing. We don't need to go to the cops. We can go to her. We can see to her in our own way. / We can make sure that she's okay. We can make sure that she gets what she needs.

DAISY: Jesus Christ.

LUCY: And Cal?

PETE: I'll talk to him.

LUCY: Pete.

PETE: I'm gonna talk to him.

LIZ: So, you see? It doesn't have to be one way or the other.

LUCY: But I was there, Liz, what does that, what does that make me? If I don't fix this…?

LIZ: Lucy, do you want to know how you fix this? You make sure that nobody else gets hurt because of what that asshole did to her. That's how you fix this. *(Beat)* Anything else is just selfish.

ROB: All in favor?

(DAISY raises her hand.)

ROB: All opposed?

(Everybody else raises their hands, even, after a moment, LUCY and MALCOLM. They put their hands down, everybody's looking at DAISY. Beat)

DAISY: So, what, was I in the room, too? *(Beat)* I mean, I wasn't at the party, but, maybe I was in the room. Hey, maybe I'm Cal?

APRIL: Daisy?

DAISY: No, you know what, maybe we should check, maybe we should just watch the video and check, although, no, you know what, we can't watch the video because if we watch the video, then we're involved, aren't we?

LIZ: Daisy, listen.

DAISY: No, but seriously, though, what's it gonna be because there has to be something, right? Hey, can you bribe me? Liz, you look pretty rich, do you want to bribe me? It wouldn't work, but.

LIZ: Fuck yourself, Daisy.

DAISY: Hey, I'm trying to help you, here. I'm on your side. Because here's the thing, you are involved now. All of you. You are the story now. And if the cameras and the news trucks arrive, they're not just gonna be looking for Cal or Laura Heller anymore, they're gonna be looking for you. So you need to put a stop to this. So, what haven't we tried? Come on, let's really put our heads into this. Do I have a problem of some kind? Could you blackmail me? Do I have a baby in a shoebox somewhere?

APRIL: Daisy...

DAISY: Or, hey, do you know what I just thought of? There's nine of you. Why don't you just beat the shit out of me? What. Now everybody's all quiet. Have I offended you? Have I offended you, Pete? You wouldn't do something like that, is that it? You're one of the good guys, right?

ROB: You know what?

DAISY: Or actually, and I really don't know why I didn't think of this sooner, Rob, maybe you should call up your old friend Cal and see if he has any suggestions for what to do with a woman when she doesn't want to do what you tell her to do? I'll bet he's got some fucking fantastic suggestions. Why don't we call him, or hey, better yet, why don't you call him, April, and then when he says something you don't wanna hear, you can hang up on him, too. How does that sound?

LIZ: Okay, and so what's your plan, here, exactly?

DAISY: My plan?

LIZ: I mean, not that it isn't refreshing to hear you talk about how awful me and all my friends are, but you aren't walking out of here with that camera, you've gotta know that by now. You could go to the police, with no evidence, but guess what, Daisy, you weren't in that room. You weren't at that party. You don't go to school here. And oh, yeah, you couldn't pick Cal Summers or Laura Heller out of a lineup, so what in the hell do you think you're gonna tell them?

DAISY: I'm gonna tell them the truth. I'm gonna tell them that a guy named Cal Summers raped a kid named Laura Heller at a party and that six days later, nine of his very best friends got together and they decided, collectively, that they didn't give a shit / because she was different.

LIZ: That's just not true.

DAISY: Because she was weird, she was annoying, or awkward, she wore the wrong clothes or had the audacity to go to a fucking lacrosse game when you didn't invite her, I'm gonna tell them that Cal Summers may have raped this girl, but his friends were the ones who buried her. And I don't need a video to do that, do I, Liz? Do I? I'm gonna tell them the truth.

APRIL: Which would have to include me, right?

DAISY: *(Beat)* It doesn't have to.

APRIL: But that's how it is, now, I'm one of them? Right? Is that it?

DAISY: April, I'm not the bad guy, here.

APRIL: Do you honestly still believe there's a bad guy here? Because there isn't. There's just kids, scared out of their fucking minds trying to take care of the people they're supposed to take care of.

DAISY: What? Like Liz? You're gonna take care of her, too, is that it, April? You're gonna, what, you're gonna make sure that she "gets what she needs." Is that it?

APRIL: Maybe. Yes.

DAISY: Well, what if she what she needs to is to go to the cops? What if what she needs is to see this fucker arrested? What will you say to her, then? Will you say it was a mistake, that Cal is a good guy, that he wouldn't mean to do anything like this?

APRIL: Daisy.

DAISY: Will you say he isn't a bad guy?!

APRIL: I DON'T KNOW OKAY I DON'T KNOW
WHAT I'D SAY. I don't know what I'm supposed to
do I don't know if what he did if he knew what he
was doing when he was doing it I don't know, Daisy,
I don't know what the right thing to do is. But if it's a
choice between believing in him and not then I have to
believe in him. I have to. And maybe that's a mistake, I
don't know, but what I do know is this, if you do this,
if you bring this to the cops, you're not just doing it to
them. You're doing it to me. Them you can hate, fine,
but this is me. You know me. You do know me, Daisy.
You know me better than anyone, like I know you, and
I know I'm not gonna talk you out of this, so. So fine.
Here.

(APRIL *walks over to* SARAH.)

ROB: April, what are you doing?

APRIL: Give it to me.

LIZ: April.

APRIL: Sarah, just.

(APRIL *snatches the bag off of* SARAH's *back and walks over
to* DAISY *as:*)

LIZ: April, what are you doing?

APRIL: Here.

(APRIL *takes out the camera and holds it out to* DAISY.)

DAISY: What in the fuck is this?

APRIL: This is what you wanted, right?

ROB: April, what are you --?

APRIL: You wanted this so you can do the right thing?
Well, maybe it is the right thing, I don't know. And if
you want to do it, I won't stop you, and neither will
anyone else. But if you go to the police, you were right,
they are going to come for us. They're gonna come for

me, and I don't know what happens next. To them. To
me. To Laura. I don't know. It scares the hell out of me,
to be honest, but I'm not gonna stop you. You want
to do it, you go right ahead. If you think it's the right
thing. Then I trust you, Daisy. I trust you with my life.
(Beat) So, what's it gonna be?

(DAISY considers the camera in APRIL's hand.)

DAISY: *(Pleading)* It's wrong. It's just wrong. And you
know that.

*(APRIL doesn't retract the camera. Beat. DAISY turns and
starts getting her shit together. Furious)*

DAISY: You know something, April, I had a best friend
this one time, she woulda kicked your ass, you know
that?

APRIL: Daisy.

(And DAISY exits, slamming the door as she goes. Beat)

ROB: So, what does that mean?

APRIL: It means it's done.

ROB: You're sure.

APRIL: You're an idiot, Rob.

LIZ: I'll do it. *(Beat)* I'll do it.

*(APRIL hands LIZ the camera. LIZ takes out the memory
card and snaps it in half. Beat. Nobody knows what to do.
NATALIE stumbles, a little.)*

PETE: *(Re: NATALIE)* We should get her to a bed.

ROB: You guys need a hand with that?

PETE: No.

ROB: Pete.

PETE: You should probably go on to the party now,
Rob.

ROB: Are you serious? *(Beat)* Liz? *(Beat. He starts getting his shit together.)* Guess you guys really needed a bad guy, huh? *(And he's gone.)*

MALCOLM: You ready to go?

LIZ: We'll talk next week, okay, Lucy?

LUCY: I'll see you guys.

(LUCY exits and MALCOLM follows).

LIZ: Maggie, you want me to—

MAGGIE: I should probably—

LIZ: Yeah, but.

MAGGIE: I'll see you tomorrow or something, Liz. *(She exits.)*

PETE: You ready?

LIZ: Yeah.

NATALIE: Hey, did you guys hear? I'm gonna be a lawyer.

LIZ: That's wonderful, baby.

(They exit. APRIL tidies, not looking at SARAH.)

SARAH: Well, that happened fast. *(Beat)* Snow's probably getting pretty bad, I should probably— *(Beat)* You know, I didn't mean for everything to—

APRIL: Of course you did.

SARAH: April.

APRIL: Of course you did.

SARAH: *(Beat)* Well. I should probably—

APRIL: *(She stops.)* Can I ask you a question?

SARAH: Yeah?

APRIL: You're friends with Laura, right?

SARAH: Yeah…?

APRIL: Why didn't you just... *(Beat)* I mean, did you call me because... *(Beat)* Why didn't you just call her?

SARAH: Why didn't you? *(Beat)* I should probably get going. The snow.

APRIL: Get home safe.

SARAH: You too.

(SARAH exits. APRIL shuts off the light. She heads for the door when her phone starts ringing again. APRIL stops, considers the phone. It rings and rings. Blackout)

END OF PLAY

CPSIA information can be obtained
at www.ICGtesting.com
Printed in the USA
FFOW04n1839270716
26109FF